WORLD OF
MAMMALS

KANGAROOS

by Peter Murray

Content Adviser: Barbara E. Brown, Associate, Mammal Division, The Field Museum, Chicago, IL

THE CHILD'S WORLD®, CHANHASSEN, MINNESOTA

KANGAROOS

Published in the United States of America by The Child's World®
PO Box 326 • Chanhassen, MN 55317-0326 • 800-599-READ • www.childsworld.com

Acknowledgements:

The Child's World®: Mary Berendes, Publishing Director

Editorial Directions, Inc.: E. Russell Primm, Editorial Director; Pam Rosenberg, Editor; Judith Shiffer, Assistant Editor; Matt Messbarger, Editorial Assistant; Susan Hindman, Copy Editor; Emily Dolbear, Proofreader; Judith Frisbie and Olivia Nellums, Fact Checkers; Tim Griffin/IndexServ, Indexer; Cian Loughlin O'Day, Photo Researcher, Linda S. Koutris, Photo Editor

The Design Lab: Kathleen Petelinsek, Designer, Production Artist, and Cartographer

Photos:

Cover: Getty Images/Digital Vision; half title/CIP: Corbis; frontispiece: Theo Allofs/Corbis.

Interior: Theo Allofs/Corbis: 5-top right and 16, 28; Animals Animals/Earth Scenes: 5-top left and 8 (Breck P. Kent), 11 (Rowan Best), 15 (Gerard Lacz), 19 (David Fritts), 20 (Juergen and Christine Sohns), 26 (Werner Layer), 32 (Michael Fogden); Corbis: 5-bottom left and 36 (Richard T. Nowitz), 34 (Paul A. Souders); Getty Images/The Image Bank/John William Banagan: 5-middle left and 23; Martin Harvey/Corbis: 5-bottom right and 31, 24; Photodisc: 13.

Library of Congress Cataloging-in-Publication Data

Murray, Peter, 1952 Sept. 29–
  Kangaroos / by Peter Murray.
     p. cm. — (The world of mammals)
  Includes index.
  ISBN 1-59296-499-0 (library bound : alk. paper) 1. Kangaroos—Juvenile literature.
I. Title. II. World of mammals (Chanhassen, Minn.)
  QL737.M35M873 2006
  599.2′22—dc22   2005002095

TABLE OF CONTENTS

Chapter One

A Mob of Roos

It is early evening in the Australian **outback.** A wire fence stretches from horizon to horizon. Birds call back and forth, announcing the sunset. The ferocious heat of the summer day is giving way to the cool of the night. High in a grove of eucalyptus trees, a mother koala munches leaves as her infant clings to her back.

Below, in the tall grasses at the edge of the grove, a kangaroo lifts its head and sniffs the air. Its large ears turn this way and that. The kangaroo stands up on its hind legs. It is a male Eastern gray kangaroo standing 1.7 meters (5.5 feet) tall. A male kangaroo is called a boomer.

The boomer lowers himself to all fours. He moves slowly from the protection of the tall grasses. He does not hop. Propping himself on his smaller front legs and his powerful tail, he swings his hind legs forward. This is called slow-walking.

Behind him, several smaller kangaroos are rising from their grassy beds. There are sixteen females, or flyers, and three young males. Three of the flyers are carrying

Australia, New Guinea, and Tasmania are the only places
on Earth where kangaroos can be found in the wild.

baby kangaroos in their pouches. Baby kangaroos are called joeys.

The kangaroos move from the eucalyptus grove into the open, where they nibble at fresh shoots of grass and tender leaves. Gray kangaroos do most of their eating in the evening and the early morning.

Every now and then, some of the kangaroos stand up on their hind legs and scan the horizon, sniffing the air and listening for danger. Gray kangaroos have few natural enemies—Australia's larger **predators** have all gone extinct—but the "roos" are constantly on the lookout.

A gray kangaroo and her joey graze on a patch of grass.

In the distance, on the other side of the fence, a flock of sheep is grazing. The kangaroos ignore the sheep—they have been sharing the same lands for more than one hundred years.

A group of kangaroos is called a mob. A mob of Eastern gray kangaroos can have up to fifty members. With so many ears, eyes, and noses, they are safer. It is almost impossible to sneak up on a mob.

The last sliver of sun sinks beneath the horizon. The mob moves across the grassland, nibbling and chewing, occasionally sniffing. One of the joeys leaves its mother's pouch and samples a tuft of grass.

The big boomer suddenly rises to his full height. The other kangaroos in the mob stop eating. Is there a strange sound? A whiff of danger? The mother makes a clucking sound, calling her joey back to her pouch.

Suddenly, the boomer thumps the ground with his back foot and the mob explodes in every direction. The roos are not slow-walking now! Their powerful hind legs carry them swiftly across the grassland in 6-meter (20-ft) leaps. The fence is no barrier—to a kangaroo, jumping over a 1.5-meter (5-ft) fence is like stepping over a curb. In an instant, the mob has scattered.

A few seconds later, a jeep comes rumbling slowly

along. A rancher is checking his fence line. He saw the mob of kangaroos bounding off, but it is no big deal. He sees roos every day. There are millions of them.

A few hundred kilometers to the north, a group of smaller kangaroos is grazing in a clearing. It is a group of rare bridled nailtail wallabies.

Once common in eastern Australia, bridled nailtail wallabies are now endangered, as are many small kangaroo **species.** One reason is that nailtails were once hunted for their beautiful pelts, but today they are protected by law. Still, with only a few hundred left in a little area of central Queensland, the species struggles to survive. Hawks, eagles, foxes, wildcats, and dingoes all prey on small kangaroos. Many species, such as the beautiful crescent nailtail, are now extinct.

A

Australia, New Guinea, and Tasmania are home to about sixty kangaroo species, from the 2-meter (6.6-ft) tall red kangaroo, to the agile tree kangaroo, to the tiniest musky rat kangaroo. Kangaroos can be found in rain forests, on desert plains, and just about everywhere in between.

Why are there millions of Eastern

gray kangaroos but only a handful of bridled nailtail wallabies? Why are rat kangaroos so small, and why do tree kangaroos live in trees? How did kangaroos evolve, and what does the future hold for them?

Bridled nailtail wallabies were once hunted for their fur. Today, they are preyed upon by dingoes, foxes, and untamed cats.

Chapter Two

What Is a Kangaroo?

Do you know what a kangaroo looks like? Big feet, huge back legs, long tail, and a face that's a cross between a horse and a dog, right?

Not exactly! Not all kangaroos look alike. Some live high in the treetops and look like long-nosed monkeys, while others nest in rocky crevices and look more like rats. But all kangaroos share certain characteristics.

MARSUPIALS

Kangaroos are marsupials. Marsupials are mammals that typically carry their young in a pouch after giving birth. There are more than 260 species of marsupials, including about 60 species of kangaroos. Most of the mammals living in Australia, New Guinea, and Tasmania are marsupials. Examples include kangaroos, koalas, opossums, Tasmanian devils, bandicoots, and wombats. A few marsupials also live in North America and South America.

Scientists believe that marsupials

Would You Believe?
In North America, the Virginia opossum is the only native marsupial.

evolved about 85 million years ago, when dinosaurs still walked the earth. Over tens of millions of years, other mammals replaced the marsupials in most parts of the world. But Australia was separated from the other continents by hundreds of miles of ocean. Marsupials continued to evolve without competition from other mammals.

Koalas are marsupials which feed on certain kinds of eucalyptus leaves.

BIG FOOT

The scientific name for kangaroo is *macropod*. In Greek, *macro* means "big" and *pod* means "foot." A kangaroo's powerful back legs and long, thin feet are key to its survival.

Kangaroos travel by hopping on their hind legs. Strong muscles are attached to thick, elastic **tendons** that give their legs plenty of "spring." Each time the kangaroo lands, its tendons stretch like giant rubber bands. The tendons then snap back, sending the roo flying through the air. Large kangaroos can leap more than 10 meters (33 ft) in a single bound and have been known to jump over fences 3 meters (10 ft) high.

A kangaroo can use its remarkable hopping ability to travel long distances quickly. A red kangaroo can travel at a speed of 40 kilometers (25 miles) per hour for more than an hour. If it is being chased, it can reach speeds of up to 70 kilometers (43 mi) per hour!

The hind feet of a large roo can measure 50 centimeters (20 inches) long. Each foot has four sharp claws. The large middle toe takes most of the roo's weight when it hops, and the large claw can be used for self-defense.

A group of red kangaroos hops across a field.

mammals have tails, which they use in different ways. Cattle use their tails to swat away biting flies. Squirrels use their furry tails to balance themselves and to keep warm. Some monkeys use their **prehensile** tails to hold on to branches.

Kangaroos use their tails for balance, slow-walking, and fighting. In slow-walking, the tail is used as a fifth leg. When a roo is hopping, its tail helps it change direction—even in midair. And when a kangaroo fights, it can balance its entire weight on its tail, leaving all four legs free for kicking and clawing.

The smaller members of the kangaroo family have found another use for their tails. Some rat kangaroos, potoroos, and bettongs use their tails to carry bundles of grass, leaves, and twigs to their nesting sites.

SENSES

Like other grazing mammals, kangaroos constantly use their senses to look for danger. Their long ears turn in every direction, listening for the quiet creeping of a predator. Their sensitive noses constantly sniff the air. Their eyes scan the horizon. Anything out of the ordinary will send a roo hopping for safety.

Would You Believe?
Because kangaroos are most active after dark, their eyes are best adapted to seeing at night.

Chapter Three

Pocket Babies

A mob of kangaroos has one **dominant** male, called the old man. The old man is usually the largest kangaroo in the group. He is the only male to **mate** with the females.

The old man must sometimes battle other males to keep his status in the group. When two kangaroos fight,

Two male red kangaroos box, or fight, each other.

they rear back on their hind legs and grapple with their front legs, trying to knock each other over. When a fight gets serious, a boomer will use its tail to support his weight

Winning fights with other male kangaroos is how male kangaroos prove their dominance.

as he kicks at his opponent with his hind feet. Usually these battles are over quickly—the smaller roo gives up and hops off. But kangaroos are strong and their claws are sharp, and occasionally the fights turn deadly.

The old man mates with all the females in his mob except those that are too young or are already pregnant. Gray kangaroos mate in the spring and summer. About five weeks after mating, the female gives birth to a single joey.

Kangaroo babies, like all marsupials, are very small. A newborn gray kangaroo is only about 2.5 centimeters (1 in) long. When it emerges from the birth canal, the blind, hairless joey must make the most important journey of its life. Using its sharp, tiny claws, the joey crawls up its mother's belly to her pouch opening. The hungry joey crawls into the warm, moist pouch and uses its sense of smell to find one of the mother's **teats.** For the next few months, the joey's mouth stays attached to the teat, feeding on its mother's rich milk.

When it is about four months old, the joey pokes his head out of the pouch for the first time. The joey doesn't leave the pouch for another month or two, but it watches and listens to the other kangaroos in the mob. It starts learning what to eat, what to fear, and how to behave.

One day, the joey climbs out of the pouch. It looks like a smaller version of its mother. It has such big feet and such a long tail, one wonders how it ever fit inside.

The joey, however, doesn't stay out long. It nibbles a tuft of grass, takes a few wobbly hops, and then dives headfirst back into the pouch. For the next two to three months, the joey spends most of its time in the pouch.

Young roos always have to keep a lookout for predators. Dingoes, foxes, and eagles are an ever-present threat. A single warning cluck from its mother or the sound of a boomer thumping his foot to warn of danger will send the joey leaping into its mother's pouch.

After about ten months, it's time for the joey to leave the pouch for good. The mother roo is ready to give birth to a new baby. But the joey's childhood is not over. It will stay close to its mother for another six to eight months. During this time, the joey will continue to poke its head inside the pouch to drink milk, even while its tiny younger brother or sister is in there attached to a teat.

By the time a joey is eighteen months old, it has become an adult. By that age, females are ready to mate and raise joeys of their own. Young males begin to **spar** with each other, practicing

Would You Believe?
When danger threatens, a female kangaroo can tighten the top of her pouch to keep her joey safe inside. If the joey is too big and danger is near, a female will relax the muscles of her pouch and let the joey flop out onto the ground where he will remain. That way, she can run away much faster and return for her joey later.

for the day when they might get big and strong enough to become the old man of the mob and father joeys of their own.

A kangaroo usually gives birth to one joey at a time.

Would You Believe?
When a kangaroo is nursing both a newborn joey and an older joey, her body produces two kinds of milk to meet their different nutritional needs.

Chapter Four

Kangaroo Types

The largest and most familiar kangaroos include six species: the Eastern gray kangaroo, the Western gray kangaroo, the red kangaroo, the common wallaroo, the antilopine wallaroo, and the black wallaroo.

The coat of a male red kangaroo (left) is much redder than the coat of a female red kangaroo (right). The female's coat has more bluish gray fur.

EASTERN AND WESTERN GRAY KANGAROOS

Gray kangaroos are found in eastern and southwestern Australia. These large roos prefer to live in mixed woodlands and grasslands. They are often seen on farms and ranches, where they compete with domestic livestock such as cows and sheep for food.

Male gray kangaroos can grow to 1.8 meters (6 ft) tall and weigh more than 70 kilograms (154 pounds). Female grays are about two-thirds the size of the males. Most gray kangaroos are grayish in color but can vary from reddish brown to almost white.

RED KANGAROOS

At more than 2 meters (6.5 ft) tall and weighing up to 90 kilograms (198 lbs), the male red kangaroo is the largest living marsupial. The red male kangaroo has a reddish brown coat while the female red kangaroo usually has a blueish gray coat. Red kangaroos are desert dwellers, living deep in the **arid** outback and traveling great distances for food and water.

WALLAROOS

The common wallaroo, or euro, is the most widespread of the large kangaroos. This shaggy-haired roo can be found

in nearly every part of Australia. Common wallaroos range in color from dark gray to pale reddish brown. They stand about 1.5 meters (5 ft) tall and weigh up to 60 kilograms (132 lbs).

Common wallaroos like to keep to themselves. They don't gather in groups like the larger kangaroos. Days

*Wallaroos have a bare, black snout. This characteristic
helps distinguish them from other kangaroos.*

are spent resting in rocky areas where caves, overhanging rocks, and ledges provide shade. Like most kangaroos, the common wallaroo comes out to feed at night.

The antilopine wallaroo is slightly smaller and more slender than the gray kangaroos. They live in the open rain forests of northern Australia. Unlike other wallaroos, the antilopine wallaroo prefers to live in groups.

The smallest and stockiest of the large kangaroos, black wallaroos are only about 1 meter (3.3 ft) tall. These shy, secretive roos are seen only in a remote, rocky area of northern Australia. Little is known of their habits.

WALLABIES

Wallabies are small kangaroos, usually weighing less than 20 kilograms (44 lbs). Australia is home to about thirty different wallaby species.

Nailtail wallabies are known for the small, horny nail at the tips of their tails. No one knows how this "nail tail" evolved or how the wallabies might use it. The Northern nailtail is common in northern Australia. The bridled nailtail is only found in one small area of Queensland and is considered endangered. The crescent nailtail wallaby has been extinct since the 1940s.

Rock wallabies are common in most parts of Australia.

Some of the many different species are brightly colored. Others have distinctive markings. True to their name, these nimble roos live in rocky areas. Some species live in large colonies of several hundred individuals.

Pademelons are small, forest-dwelling wallabies. Several species inhabit the coastal forests of southern and eastern Australia. Pademelons have smaller tails than other wallabies.

The yellow-footed rock wallaby is just one of about thirty different kinds of wallabies found in Australia.

Hare-wallabies got their name because they look something like rabbits. These tiny wallabies usually weigh less than 2 kilograms (4.4 lbs). They live in the open grasslands of northern and western Australia. Over the past century, hare-wallabies have suffered from loss of **habitat.** Non-native predators such as foxes and wildcats have driven two of the five species to extinction.

TREE KANGAROOS

In the rain forests of New Guinea, you would probably see an animal in the trees that looked like a cross between a small bear and a monkey. This is a tree kangaroo. These tree-dwelling creatures look nothing like the big, bounding, grass-eating roos of Australia. The tree kangaroo has smaller hind legs, larger front legs, a tail that is longer than its body, and short, furry ears.

Tree kangaroos are built for climbing, but they are still kangaroos. Using their powerful hind legs, they can leap more than 10 meters (33 ft) from tree to tree. At times, a tree kangaroo will wrap its front legs around a trunk and use its hind legs to hop up the tree.

There are ten known species of tree

Would You Believe?
The tammar wallaby, found only on some small islands off the south coast of Australia, is one of the few mammals that can drink saltwater without getting sick.

kangaroo. Eight live in New Guinea and two live in the northern rain forests of Australia.

RAT KANGAROOS

These tiniest members of the kangaroo family range from the size of a rat to the size of a rabbit. Rat kangaroos are common in many parts of Australia, but two of the nine known species are now extinct, and others are endangered.

Rat kangaroos have the most varied diets of all the roos. They eat fruit, grass, insects, animal bones, mushrooms, roots, and just about anything else they can catch or chew. Their tails are relatively thinner than those of larger roos. When rat kangaroos hop, their tails drag on the ground.

Bettongs are the largest member of the rat kangaroo family. The rufous bettong of eastern Australia weighs about 3 kilograms (6.6 lbs).

Potoroos are long-nosed rat kangaroos that live in the moist forests and scrublands of the southern Australia coast

Would You Believe?
The largest of the tree-dwelling roos, Bennett's tree kangaroo is about 1.5 meters (5 ft) long and weighs about 13 kilograms (29 lbs).

Would You Believe?
Most rat kangaroos have prehensile tails. That means they can use their tail like a fifth limb. When building their nests, rat kangaroos use their tails to carry bundles of grass and leaves to their nesting sites.

and the island of Tasmania. Of the three known potoroo
species, one is extinct and one is very rare.

The smallest of all kangaroos, the musky rat kangaroo
weighs only about 0.5 kilogram (1.1 lbs). Its small size

Tree kangaroos don't look much like other kangaroos.

and long, naked tail make it look more like a rat than a kangaroo. It is the only kangaroo that does not hop as its main way of getting around—it usually walks like other animals. It is also the only kangaroo that frequently gives birth to twins.

The musky rat kangaroo lives in the rain forests of northeastern Australia.

Chapter Five

Roos and People

People and kangaroos first met more than 40,000 years ago when the first humans landed on the shores of Australia. Those early **aborigines** saw kangaroos as a source of food. The largest kangaroo back then was *Procoptodon goliah,* a 3-meter (9.8-ft) tall, 200-kilogram (440-lb) giant. This enormous kangaroo probably fed on tree leaves. The aborigines looked at *Procoptodon* and saw a feast!

Procoptodon goliah soon became extinct, probably because of hunting by humans. The other large kangaroo species did better. For tens of thousands of years, humans and kangaroos lived in balance. Though humans hunted kangaroos for their meat, bones, and hides, kangaroos reproduce quickly. There was plenty of space, and the kangaroos' native habitat remained mostly undisturbed.

Then in the late 1700s, Europeans began to colonize Australia in large numbers. Over the next two centuries, huge areas of Australian wilderness were converted to farms and ranches. Instead of dodging the handmade spears and boomerangs of the aborigines, kangaroos now

faced shotguns and rifles. The European colonists killed kangaroos for meat and for sport. They also killed kangaroos to protect their newly planted crops.

An Aboriginal painting found in Kakadu National Park in Australia shows a man hunting a kangaroo

Remarkably, the larger kangaroos have increased in number since the European invasion. Although they have been heavily hunted, the big roos benefit from the grasses and other crops planted by farmers, and from the water that is piped into desert areas for irrigation and livestock. Today, red and gray kangaroos are so numerous they are considered pests in some areas.

The smaller kangaroos—tree kangaroos, wallabies, and rat kangaroos—have been hit hard by the arrival of the Europeans. The tree kangaroos of New Guinea and northern Australia have few natural enemies, but they are now threatened because their rain forests are being cut down for lumber or cleared for farmland.

Human hunters, the loss of habitat, and the hungry wildcats and foxes brought by Europeans threaten wallaby species. Some species of hare-wallabies are now extinct due to these animals, and wild goats compete for food and shelter in the rocky areas where rock wallabies live.

The smallest kangaroos—rat kangaroos, potoroos,

Would You Believe?
In the Australian outback, collisions between motor vehicles and kangaroos are common—about 20,000 every year. Many drivers install "roo bars" on their front bumpers to protect their cars from damage.

Would You Believe?
The toolache wallaby, a particularly graceful and attractive species, was hunted for its beautiful hide. It became extinct in the 1920s.

A rancher bottle-feeds a baby kangaroo. Many people
are working to preserve endangered kangaroo species.

Would You Believe?
The only kangaroo to live in underground burrows, the burrowing bettong or boodie, is now extinct on mainland Australia because of hunting by foxes. Boodies survive on only a few islands where there are no foxes.

and bettongs—have suffered greatly from loss of habitat and from hunting by cats and foxes. They also must compete with other European imports, including rabbits, rats, and mice, for food and shelter. Many of these small kangaroos are now extinct, while others survive on only a few islands where foxes and cats have not been introduced.

Some small kangaroo species are probably doomed to extinction. But the people of Australia and New Guinea are working to save as many species as possible. The hunting of kangaroos is now strictly regulated. Large kangaroos are still hunted for their meat and hides, but only in areas where they are present in large numbers.

Efforts are also being made to preserve kangaroo habitat and to establish reserves where roos can live and breed without being hunted, trapped, or run over by trucks. With a little help, kangaroos are likely to survive into the next century and beyond.

Glossary

aborigines (ab-uh-RIJ-uh-neez) the native people of Australia who lived there before the arrival of Europeans

arid (AIR-id) extremely dry

dominant (DOM-uh-nuhnt) strongest or most powerful

habitat (HAB-uh-tat) the place and condition in which an animal lives

incisors (in-SI-zurz) sharp, front teeth used for cutting

mate (MAYT) to join together to produce offspring

molars (MO-lurz) large, flat teeth at the back of the mouth that are used for grinding

outback (OUT-bak) the isolated, rural part of Australia

predators (PRED-uh-turz) animals that hunt other animals for food

prehensile (pree-HEN-suhl) made for grabbing or gripping by wrapping around an object

spar (SPAHR) to fight

species (SPEE-sheez) a group of animals that share certain characteristics

teats (TEETS) the part of a female animal's body from which its young drink milk

tendons (TEN-duhnz) strong bands of tissue that connect muscles to bones or other body parts

For More Information

Watch It

Australia's Kangaroos. DVD (Washington, D.C., National Geographic, 2000).

Kangaroos: Faces in the Mob. DVD (Silver Spring, Md., Acorn Media, 2000).

Read It

Eckart, Edana. *Red Kangaroo*. Danbury, Conn.: Children's Press, 2003.

Green, Jen. *Kangaroos*. Danbury, Conn.: Grolier Educational, 2001.

Lantier, Patricia, Judith Logan Lehne, and John F. McGee (illustrator). *The Wonder of Kangaroos*. Milwaukee: Gareth Stevens Publishing, 2001.

Miller, Chuck. *Tree Kangaroos*. Austin, Tex.: Steadwell Books, 2002.

Penny, Malcolm. *Kangaroo: Habitat, Life Cycles, Food Chains, Threats*. Austin, Tex.: Raintree Steck-Vaughn, 2004.

Look It Up

Visit our home page for lots of links about kangaroos: *http://www.childsworld.com/links*

Note to Parents, Teachers, and Librarians: We routinely verify our Web links to make sure they are safe, active sites—so encourage your readers to check them out!

The Animal Kingdom
Where Do Kangaroos Fit In?

Kingdom: Animal

Phylum: Chordates (animals with backbones)

Class: Mammalia (animals that feed their young milk)

Order: Metatheria (marsupials)

Families: Macropodidae (kangaroos and wallabies) and Potoroidae (bettongs, potoroos, and rat kangaroos)

Index

About the Author
Peter Murray has written more than eighty children's books on science, nature, history, and other topics. An animal lover, Pete lives in Golden Valley, Minnesota, in a house with one woman, two poodles, several dozen spiders, thousands of microscopic dust mites, and an occasional mouse.